SANBORN
ON
SUCCESS

The Griffin Distilled Wisdom Series
Griffin Publishing

First Edition 1996
10 9 8 7 6 5 4 3 2

ISBN1-882180-50-X

Published by
Griffin Publishing
544 West Colorado Street
Glendale California 91204
(818) 244-2128 (818) 242-1172 Fax
Manufactured in the United States of America

Sanborn on Success

For successful people, there are at least two major challenges. The first is to become the best. The second is, once you've become the best, to keep getting better. The second challenge may be even more difficult than the first.

Ideas are the seeds of greatness. I've tried to collect some of the best quotes about success in this book and I've added my own reflections and insights about each. My purpose is to provide you with both the stimulation and motivation to achieve more success in life and to become all that you are capable of being. That, too, is my personal desire.

I hope this book is a useful tool in your quest to become the best and to keep getting better.

1

*Times may change but
truth is timeless.*

—*Mark Sanborn*

The fundamentals of success in any endeavor are timeless. Techniques and technologies may change, but the underlying principles remain the same. Great truths are the foundation of a successful life and career.

2

It's a funny thing about life: If you refuse to accept anything but the very best you will very often get it.

—W. Somerset Maugham

Our expectations powerfully shape our destinies. While a few may aim too high, it is the greater tragedy that most aim too low. They underestimate their ability to pursue and achieve great things. Do you expect each day to be filled with excitement and opportunity? If you do, you probably experience more than those who expect only drudgery and monotony.

3

He who has a reason why can bear most any how.

—*Frederick Wilhelm Nietszche*

Goals don't necessarily motivate you. A goal without a reason to achieve it is useless. Ask yourself why you are pursuing certain goals. Are your reasons powerful?

One of the most important questions you can hope to answer in your life is this: *Why do you live?* What is your compelling purpose in life? Purpose is the beginning point of greatness.

4

*Never postpone happiness or waste
the present by living in the past.*

—*Mark Sanborn*

The past can serve to educate (if
we learn from it), encourage (if
we let past successes bolster our
confidence for the future) or entertain
(if we remember the good times and
people we've met). But the past is an
unsuitable place to live. We have
only the present moment to live.
And if we live it well, we are assured
of a positive past.

5

Luck favors momentum.

—unknown

One of my earliest mentors told me to rob a few gas stations on the way to robbing the bank. He wasn't, of course, advocating a life of crime. He was using a powerful metaphor: Little attempts and successes prepare us for bigger challenges.

6

Rule 1: Whatever happens is normal.
Be flexible. Use change.

—Joe Calloway

Successful people are adaptable, not rigid. When circumstances change, they change their behavior to maximize the outcome. Because nothing stays the same, just assume whatever happens is "normal," then choose the best possible response.

7

If I didn't make so many mistakes, I wouldn't be so smart.

—*Rhoda Olsen*

What is your paradigm of mistakes? Here's a healthy perspective: Mistakes are needed lessons in our education. Rather than belabor a mistake, ask yourself what you've learned from it.

Of course learning shouldn't take too many lessons. As a CEO once told one of his managers, "Make a mistake and I'll figure you were trying something new. Make the same mistake twice and I'll fire you for being a slow learner."

8

*There's nothing lost and much to be
gained by admitting
that you're human.*

—W. Steven Brown

The inability to admit a mistake kills
credibility. You can't legitimately take
responsibility for your successes if you
don't also accept responsibility for your
mistakes.

9

Do not imagine yourself to be less than you are, nor more than you are, but seek always to become all of which you are capable.

—*Jim Rohn*

One of the saddest excuses for poor behavior or performance is, "I was just being myself—that's the way I am." Leaders focus on the way they can be, not on any natural inclination to mediocrity. Are you striving to be yourself—or your *best* self?

10

Adversity sharpens us.

—unknown

Nobody would volunteer to be "sharpened." But it consoles us to know that despite the unpleasantness of adversity, it hones our character and develops our skills.

11

*Choose your rut carefully. You'll be
in it a long time.*

—sign on a muddy road

The primary difference between a rut and a grave is depth! Sticking to familiar routines and activities deprives us of the diversity of life. Make it a point to try something new—a food, activity or even the way you drive to work—each day. If you can't stay out of a rut, at least redirect it!

Decision making is easy when values are clear.

—*Roy Disney*

The bad news: You can't have it all. The good news: When your values are clear and you know what's important, you don't want it all anyway. The most fulfilled and motivated people are those who live their values.

The Distilled Wisdom Series

13

*Argue for your limitations and
they're yours.*

—*Richard Bach*

Like expectations, our limitations are often self-imposed. As we tell others about what can't be done, we convince ourselves of what we can't do.

14

If you walk, just walk. If you sit, just sit. But whatever you do, don't wobble.

—Master Ummon

Motivated people live life boldy. Whatever they do, they do decisively. Hesitation and uncertainty rob us of energy and power. Are you committed in everything you do?

15

*Just because a skier falls down
doesn't mean he isn't a skier.*

—*Devany McNeill*

Failing isn't failure. Ultimate failure is when we stop trying. As a skier I can assure you that if you don't fall down occasionally, you are neither learning nor challenging yourself.

16

*You ain't going nowhere, son. You
ought to go back to driving a truck.*

> —*Told to Elvis Presley after his
> first performance at the
> Grand Ole Opry*

So much for the advice of others.
What you believe you can do is more
important than what others believe
you can do.

17

*When things are bad, keep going.
Your experience and skills will bring
you back.*

—*Michael McKinley*

Perseverance is a characteristic of the motivated. You can win most contests in life by simply staying the course after others have given up.

18

*What you learn is more important
than what you earn.*

—*Jim Rohn*

And what you earn is a function of
what you've learned. Money is a way
of keeping score. The knowledge
you acquire is yours for a lifetime. It
can never be stolen, taxed or taken
away.

19

*...the reason that we exist must surely
be for each other.*

—*Albert Einstein*

The quality of our lives is directly related to the quality of our relationships. Are you adding to, or taking away from, the lives of others?

20

If you keep doing what you've always done, you'll keep getting what you've always gotten.

—unknown

Insanity, it has been said, is doing what you've always done and expecting different results. Motivated people know that if they want different results, they must do different things. Maybe it's time to change your approach.

The Distilled Wisdom Series

21

If you believe in nothing, honey, it believes in you.

—Robyn Hitchcock

What do you believe in? Bankruptcy is rooted in a lack of belief. It is difficult for others to believe in you if you do not believe in yourself. And only the hardened cynic no longer believes in other people. Do this: Make a list of your 10 most important core beliefs about life. Review your list to determine what new beliefs you want to develop and what existing beliefs you need to bolster.

22

*Probably the greatest harm done by
vast wealth is the harm that we of
moderate means do to ourselves when
we let the vices of envy and hatred
enter deep into our own natures.*

—Theodore Roosevelt

Let the wealth and success of others
inspire you rather than intimidate you.
No amount of envy will improve your
own situation. Substitute the energy of
action for the envy of others.

23

Among your affairs there should be no more than two or three matters of great concern.

—*Hagakure*

In the course of a typical day, you and I probably do dozens of different things. But if at the end of the day you reflect on what your activities accomplished, you may find that two or three things made the biggest difference. Learn to separate the significant from the trivial.

There is no wealth but life.

—John Ruskin

As long as you are alive, you have hope. Every blessing flows from the gift of life.

25

The human mind: You can't forget to take it with you but you can forget to use it.

—*Mark Sanborn*

We need to be mindful—consciously aware of what's going on around us and how to best create and/or interact with our circumstances.

Showing up is 80 percent of life.

—*Woody Allen*

Nothing can happen if you don't show up. If you want to make things happen, show up more often. (But be prepared when you get there.)

27

*Is life not a hundred times too short
for us to bore ourselves?*

—*Friedrich Wilhelm Nietszche*

And if life were a hundred times longer, it would still be a drag to be bored. Boredom or excitement are the products of choices, not circumstances.

When God closes a door
He opens a window.

—Mary Kay Ash

"No way out" is an excuse for people who have quit looking for the windows.

29

Wisdom is the principal thing:
Therefore get wisdom, and with all
thy getting get understanding.

—*Proverbs 4:7*

Organized data is information. Information understood is knowledge. But knowledge correctly applied is wisdom. Data, information and knowledge are all important, but wisdom is more important still.

Fools can learn from their own experience; the wise learn from the experience of others.

—*Democritus*

Don't repeat the mistakes you observe others have made, but emulate those actions that have made for their successes. How good are you at vicarious learning?

31

*Do the things you fear and the death
of fear will be certain.*

— unknown

Action is the antidote to worry. Doing destroys doubt. The first step, while the hardest, is probably the most important.

*People with fires in their bellies tend
to make their own luck.*

—*Lee Iaccoca*

And what is fire in the belly? It is a
burning desire to achieve and succeed.

33

If we all did the things we
are capable of doing, we would
literally astound ourselves.

—*Thomas Edison*

Your current abilities do not determine your potential capabilities. Most people are capable of much more than they ever imagine or achieve. The biggest fraud you commit is underestimating your capabilities.

Too many people see change as what other people need to do.

—*David Zach*

Until you see the need to change, you won't see the benefits. And if you don't see the benefits, you won't be willing to incur the discomfort that change requires.

35

People are always blaming their circumstances for what they are. I don't believe in circumstances. The people who get on in this world are the people who get up and look for the circumstances they want, and, if they can't find them, make them.

—*George Bernard Shaw*

Seldom do we succeed because of circumstances; usually we succeed despite them. Turn circumstances into opportunities.

Action is eloquence.

—*William Shakespeare*

Don't talk about what you're going to do, do it. Don't brag about your intentions, act. Practice the eloquence of action.

37

Information + Application =
Transformation

—Mark Sanborn

If you and I did half of what we already know, we'd probably be on a yacht right now drinking champagne. Success isn't based on what you know, but on what you do with the information.

38

*Sad will be the day for any man
when he becomes contented with the
thoughts he is thinking and the deeds
he is doing.*

—Phillips Brooks

Contentment breeds complacency
and complacency kills excellence. Be
proud of what you've accomplished,
but don't allow yourself to be content
if you are capable of doing better.

39

Geniuses aim at targets that others can't see and hit them.

—Devon Blaine

Those with vision clearly see in their minds that which others can't even imagine.

We cannot do everything at once, but we must do something at once.

—*Calvin Coolidge*

Being overwhelmed often prevents people from starting. The solution: Don't try to do it all, just start with the most important thing.

41

The majority of people are content with the least they can obtain from a meager existence, but a few brave souls demand only the best and they drive on with persistence.

— *Mark Sanborn*

When my younger brother graduated from high school many years ago, I gave him this advice: Do whatever you do better than anybody else who does it and you will succeed.

I guess I had the good fortune to be influenced by a lot of people who had very high expectations of themselves and everybody around them.

—*Randall Tobias*

Are you associating with people with high expectations? Do you seek out those with lofty ideals and big dreams? Hang out with the dreamers and schemers, not the moaners and groaners.

43

The Acorn Principle™: Your greatest, fastest and easiest growth will always come from your natural abilities.

—*Jim Cathcart*

Have you done an inventory of your personal strengths? Don't become so obsessed with your weaknesses that you overlook those things that you do well. Operate from strength rather than weakness.

44

A person all wrapped up in himself
generally makes a pretty
small package.

—E. Joseph Cossman

Self-absorption prevents us from being sensitive to others and being of service. The self-absorbed person thinks only of himself or herself.

45

We're so concerned about copying everybody else's techniques and systems that we fail to see that we're all starting to look and act alike. I don't believe that competition today has bred creativity and innovation. I believe that competition today has bred conformity.

—Steve Miller

If you act just like everybody else, you'll get the same results as everybody else. Achievers are those who are different in a positive way. They capitalize on their unique factor.

What we think, or what we know, or what we believe is, in the end, of little consequence. The only consequence is what we do.

—*John Ruskin*

It doesn't help to know something if you don't use the information. Consequences are created by actions, not analysis; by behavior, not just beliefs. What are you doing *today* that will make a difference in your life? What idea can you implement *now* to win?

47

*The unexamined life is
not worth living.*

—*Socrates*

How well do you know yourself? Understanding people begins with understanding yourself. You can't motivate yourself without understanding your motivations. And understanding your behavior is key to changing outcomes. It is dangerous to live life on autopilot.

48

We do not lack leaders. Take your pick. Various trumpets are always being sounded. We lack sufficient followers. That is always the real problem with leadership.

—Gary Wills

Who have you chosen to follow? Follow only the sound of those trumpets that ring true. You don't have enough hours in the day to adopt every cause, so choose your causes carefully. But once you commit to follow, be a dynamic follower.

49

When we are unable to find tranquility within ourselves, it is useless to seek it elsewhere.

—*La Rochefoucauld*

Tranquility and stability aren't "out there"; they're "in here." You must first make peace with yourself before you can make peace with others. The world is continually changing and shifting, so build a strong internal foundation.

*No matter how much we acquire or
fulfill our every desire, what good is
all that wealth when we've lost our
health and have to suffer
until we expire?*

—Dr. Wayne Pickering

Success can cost too much. If you've
sacrificed your health to achieve your
goals, you've paid too much.

51

*Happiness is the byproduct
of a good life.*

—*Dr. Dennis Waitley*

Somebody once said that happiness is like a butterfly: Chase it and it eludes you. But sit quietly and eventually it will land on your shoulder. In life, we don't need to sit quietly and wait for happiness; we need only to live well and happiness will come.

We usually don't do until we must do. Those who do before they must are those with the advantage.

—*Mark Sanborn*

Changing only when necessary to survive is changing too late. By then, you are changing to catch up rather than get ahead. Change before it is necessary.

53

*If character is not driving your life,
then convenience is.*

—*John Crudele*

Women and men with character do what's *right*, not what's *easy*. Their biology matches their theology.

You can be motivated by making money or by making meaning. The contemporary challenge is to do both.

—*Mark Sanborn*

There are thousands of ways to make a living in America. Are you pursuing a career that enables you to make a living and create a quality life?

55

Nothing is more confusing than people who give good advice but set bad examples.

—*Norman Vincent Peale*

Here's a mixed metaphor (but it is true): People don't hear what we say; they hear what we do. The moral of the story: If you can't practice what you preach, then don't preach!

56

You may be disappointed if you fail,
but you are doomed if you don't try.

—*Beverly Sills*

If you try and fail, you've accomplished much: You've learned to overcome fear and take a reasonable risk, you've learned something from the attempt and you've sharpened your skills. In short, our failures pave the road to success.

The Distilled Wisdom Series

57

Do not do unto others as you think they should do unto you. Their tastes may not be the same.

—*George Bernard Shaw*

Take time to understand the differences in people. Then treat them the way they want to be treated, and you'll be known as a master of human relations.

On with the dance.
Let joy be unconfined.

—*Mark Twain*

How are you moving through life? Dragging your feet or kicking your heels? Make joy a visible part of your journey.

59

*You only learn about life, reality and
the world by action.*

—*Thomas McGuane*

If there is a bias in this book, it is toward action; not rash or foolish action, but purposeful and calculated action. As the line from the old poem says, "Sitting still and wishing makes no one great. The good Lord sends the fishes, but you must cast the bait."

60

*We promise you, no Civil War
movies will ever make a nickel.*

*—What MGM said when it turned
down "Gone With The Wind"*

The problem with critics: You only
know they were wrong in retrospect.
In the present, you must follow your
convictions...despite what the critics
say. (And someday, if you're lucky,
you prove how wrong they were.)

61

You don't drown by falling in water; you drown by staying there.

—unknown

What's your rebound quotient? That is, how quickly do you get back up when you're knocked down? Learn to shorten your recovery time from setbacks.

Goals should direct us, not define us.

—Mark Sanborn

While we move towards goals, they often evolve into better ones. We shouldn't be so fixated on a goal that it prevents us from reaching a better destination.

63

*There are two kinds of failures: those
who thought and never did and those
who did and never thought.*

—unknown

People who think and never do are daydreamers and laggards while those who do and never think are imprudent fools. Those who both think and do are the achievers.

64

Plans will get you into things but you have got to work your way out.

—*Will Rogers*

How consistent is your follow-through? If you start much and complete little, you may need to reevaluate your approach.

The Distilled Wisdom Series

9/7/01

65

It is our duty as men and women to proceed as though limits to our abilities do not exist.

—Pierre Teilhard de Chardin

Live boldy, as if there were no limits. And if your encounter a barrier, treat it as only temporary.

Eliminate something superfluous from your life. Break a habit. Do something that makes you feel insecure. Carry out an action with complete attention and intensity, as if it were your last.

—*Piero Ferrucci*

Go for the adrenaline rush. Stay too comfortable for too long and you'll become numb.

67

Only those who risk going too far
will ever find out how far they can go.

—unknown

The bold are barrier bashers and limit busters. None of us really knows how good we can be or how much we can achieve, so we must keep reaching higher.

68

*I ask to be nothing more than an
ordinary human being on an
extraordinary mission.*

—Christa McAuliffe

Ordinary people pursuing extraordinary missions go down in the history books as extraordinary people.

69

*Choose your love carefully, then love
your choice.*

— unknown

There is much we can do and could do,
but we can't do it all. If you take on too
much, you'll never be able to honor
your commitments. Once you've chosen your love, then commit to it with
passion.

*The right to do something does not
mean that doing it is right.*

—*William Safire*

We have become a nation of people
obsessed with our rights but negligent
of our responsibilities. We need to ask
not if we have the right to do something,
but rather *is it the right* thing to do?

71

Make no little plans: They have no power to stir men's souls.

—*Daniel Burnham*

If your plans don't excite you, you need to make other plans.

Money never starts an idea; it is the idea that starts the money.

—*W.J. Cameron*

Money isn't a resource; it is a byproduct of how you invest your time and talents. A good idea attracts money like a magnet attracts steel.

The Distilled Wisdom Series

73

A monk entered a monastery where he was allowed to speak only two words each year. At the end of the first year, his spiritual leader asked for his comments. "Food bad," he said. The second year, his words were, "Bed cold." The third year he spoke, "I quit." "Good riddance," said his elder. "You've done nothing but complain since you came here."

If you can't say something positive, you haven't thought about it very hard. Life is full of negatives, but most people don't want to hear them rehashed. If you need catharsis, choose carefully those people you complain to.

I have learned not to act in my own
life, not to lose touch
with my real self.

—*Mel Gibson*

If you have to "fake it to make it," then the person who makes it won't really be you. The world resonates to those who are genuine.

The Distilled Wisdom Series

75

The crowded life is most easily remembered. A life full of turns, achievements, disappointments, surprises, and crisis is a life full of landmarks. The empty life has even its few details blurred and cannot be remembered with certainty.

—*Eric Hoffer*

When Hoffer refered to the "crowded life," I believe he meant a life lived fully, not one crammed with pointless activity. A hectic and busy life can still result in emptiness. Crowd your life with the *right stuff.*

76

*Take change by the hand or it will
seize you by the throat.*

—Winston Churchill

Y ou can resist change, accept it or
embrace it. Those who resist it fail.
Those who accept it get by. Those
who embrace it lead.

77

You can be sincere and still be stupid.

—Charles Kettering

Passion is important, but it must be guided by intellect. Just because someone fervently believes something doesn't make it true. The power of emotion is best guided by wisdom.

Winning big is usually preceded by failing big and often more than once.

—*Mark Sanborn*

Have you experienced any big flops lately? Failures that are real humdingers? If not, you're probably not trying the kind of things that will enable you to score big someday.

79

We are what we repeatedly do.
Excellence, then, is not an act,
but a habit.

—Aristotle

Success or failure are the culmination
of our many habits. Which direction are
your habits taking you?

The next time you're in a meeting,
look around and identify the
yes-butters and the why-notters. The
why-notters move the world.

—*Louise Pierson*

Yes-butters have a hundred reasons why the bold plan won't work. Why-notters are driven by the desire to make it work. The difference is perspective.

81

*It's better to be a "has-been" than a
"never-was."*

—*Mark Sanborn*

Some people fear success because
they aren't sure they will be able to
sustain it. There are no guarantees:
Once successful doesn't mean always
successful. But it sure beats never
successful and always trying to be.

Status quo is a myth. You're either getting better or you're getting worse.

—*Woody Hayes*

It's true: In a competitive world, the people and organizations around us continue to improve. If we stay the same, in a relative sense we're losing ground.

83

Self-actualization is the tendency of every human being to make real his or her full potential to become everything that he or she can be. The self-actualizing person is the true species-type...not a normal person with something added, but a normal person with nothing taken away.

—*George Leonard*

Drop the baggage, chip away at the excess stone, free yourself from the encumberances, and become everything you were meant to be.

Goals are dreams with deadlines.

—unknown

A dream without a deadline is little more than wishful thinking.

The Distilled Wisdom Series

85

To have faith in yourself and your ideas, that is the mark of success.

—*unknown*

It is easy to believe in yourself when everybody else does. But can you believe in yourself when others doubt and the odds are against you? You're never truly bankrupt until the day you stop believing.

Where you've been or where you are
aren't as important as where you're
going and what you're
doing to get there.

—*Mark Sanborn*

I like people who live their lives in drive, not reverse. Be a person gazing out, not looking back. Where are you headed—*right now?*

87

Money is a terrible master but an excellent servant.

— *P.T. Barnum*

What is your relationship to money? Does it control you, your time and energy? Or are you using it to increase the quality of life for yourself and your family?

I don't want to be saved.
I want to be spent.

—*Fritz Perls*

Do you know how it feels to be *used* up at the end of a day when you've invested every bit of energy in doing those things that matter most? It is an exuberant exhaustion.

The Distilled Wisdom Series

89

Enjoy the weather here. It may not be as nice where you're going.

—Advice from hotel employee as I was departing

We seldom enjoy where we're at as much as we think we're going to enjoy where we're going. To increase your enjoyment, learn to appreciate the best of where you are and what you're doing right now. Savor the moment.

Interviewer: "How do you do it?"
100-year-old man: "It's easy. You
just keep breathing."
Interviewer: "I hope to see you next
year."
100-year-old man: "No reason you
shouldn't. You look pretty
healthy to me."

As I write this, my grandfather is 89 years old. He has a keen mind and a sharp wit. Who says growing older has to diminish any aspect of our lives?

91

We may affirm absolutely that nothing great in the world has ever been accomplished without passion.

—*Georg Hegel*

To discover your personal hot buttons, ask a simple question: What am I passionate about? Either do what you're passionate about or work at becoming passionate about what you do. There is no third option.

*Always leave enough time in your life
to do something that makes you
happy, satisfied, even joyous. That
has more of an effect on economic
well-being than any other factor.*

> —*Paul Hawken*

Do something each day just for the
pure fun of it.

93

*If you chase two rabbits,
both will escape.*

—*unknown*

Trying to have it all could prevent you from having anything. Focus on what matters most.

94

*Imagination is more important
than knowledge.*

—Albert Einstein

Knowledge looks at *what is*, and as
such is bound by reality. Imagination
considers *what could be*, and knows
no limits. Stretch your brain.

The Distilled Wisdom Series

95

*Show me a thoroughly satisfied man
and I will show you a failure.*

—*Thomas Edison*

If you've become satisfied with what you're doing, direct your efforts toward something that needs to be fixed, modified, eliminated or improved. Make a list of everything that annoys or irritates you, and make it your goal to change those things. The world continually needs repair.

You only live once, but if you work it right, once is enough.

—*Joe E. Lewis*

Nothing is really "preparation for life." There is no dress rehearsal. This is it!

97

We don't choose to be role models; we are chosen. Our only choice is whether to be a good role model or a bad one.

—*Karl Malone*

How many people did you influence today? You'll never know, because many people—friends, relatives, coworkers, customers and even strangers—observe your actions. Is your example giving them something higher to aim for?

No pessimist ever discovered the secrets of the stars...or sailed to an unchartered land...or opened a new heaven to the human spirit.

—*Helen Keller*

Optimists don't deny reality; they merely choose to find the best in every situation. They concentrate on the hoped-for rather than the dreaded. They don't overlook mediocrity, but they focus on excellence.

The Distilled Wisdom Series

99

Don't confuse fame with success.
Madonna is one;
Helen Keller is the other.

—*Erma Bombeck*

Fame and fortune are functions of competency in an area of endeavor but not necessarily a function of character. Nobody should ever have to choose between competence and character when picking a role model. Leaders are those people who possess both.

*Character is what you are
in the dark.*

—Dwight L. Moody

Character is a consistency between
who you are in public and who you are
in private when nobody else is watch-
ing.

101

To be successful, the first thing to do is to fall in love with your work.

—*Sister Mary Lauretta*

If you're not doing what you like, choose to like what you're doing. How? Infuse your work with three things: fun, creativity and passion. Reinvent your work!

I like living. I have sometimes been wildly, despairingly, acutely miserable, racked with sorrow, but through it all I still know quite certainly that just to be alive is a good thing.

—Agatha Christie

Those really good at what they do get a big kick out of just being alive. Recognizing the marvel of life is the foundation of successful living.

√9\17\01

103

I shot an arrow into the air
and it stuck.

—anonymous

Ever have one of those days? Humor
helps us over the humps.

*They know enough who
know how to learn.*

—*Henry Brooks Adams*

I don't recall that anybody ever taught me how to learn, but I've decided that knowing how to learn is a critical life skill. Become a student of learning how to learn.

105

We have it in our power to begin the world all over again.

—*Thomas Paine*

Each morning life gives us a clean slate. We do not need to repeat the mistakes and disappointments of yesterday. Take advantage of the new beginnings each day offers.

I pray hard, work hard and leave the rest to God.

—*Florence Griffith Joyner*

There are challenges bigger than we are. Faith makes up for the difference in size.

107

To have meaningful work is a tremendous happiness.

—*Rita Mae Brown*

Is meaning inherent in all forms of work? I'm not sure but I do know this: We make our work meaningful by how we do it. Anyone who knows what gives their life significance is able to make their work significant.

He who has health has hope. And he who has hope has everything.

—*Arabian proverb*

As long as you breathe, you have hope. Take care of yourself. Your health is the most important thing you've got.

The Distilled Wisdom Series

109

Study as if you were going to live forever; live as if you were going to die tomorrow.

—*Marion Mitchell*

Are you smarter today than you were yesterday? I saw an 80-year-old woman on an airplane reading a little booklet on how to get along with people. She's still learning!

*No one can make you feel inferior
without your consent.*

—*Eleanor Roosevelt*

Two good ideas: First, don't let anyone put you down. (Lots of people
think that is a good idea.) Secondly,
don't put anyone else down. (Not too
many people have caught on to this
one.)

111

The tragedy of life is not that it ends so soon, but that we wait so long to begin it.

—*Richard L. Evans*

What are you waiting for? It's time to rock and roll!

*Life is not meant to be easy, my child;
but take courage: It can be delightful.*

—*George Bernard Shaw*

"Delightfully difficult"—the paradox of life.

113

People are so used to seeing what's missing, they fail to see what's there.

—unknown

Change your perspective for a moment. What good things have you overlooked?

The only losers are the ones that don't get in the race.

—W. Mitchell

If everyone seems to be passing you by, maybe it's because you simply aren't in the race.

115

To achieve real success, you must exceed peoples' expectations—including your own!

—*Tom Callister*

Our own expectations can limit us. Make it a goal to exceed yourself.

116

*There's as much risk in doing
nothing as in doing something.*

—Trammell Crow

It pays to be cautious and study a
situation before you act, but don't let
your analysis lead to paralysis.

117

He who wrestles with us strengthens our nerves, and sharpens our skills. Our antagonist is our helper.

—*Edmund Burke*

Enemies and opponents can assist us in our quest for success if we learn from our struggles with them.

When the horse is dead, get off.

—unknown

Identify the dead horses in your life: the ideas that have proven erroneous, the beliefs that hold you back, the activities that are unnecessary and unrewarding and the regrets that you keep rehearsing.

The Distilled Wisdom Series

119

I can is more important than IQ.

—*Ronald Nagrodski*

IQ is genetic but "I can" is chosen. The former is the capacity of your intellect, the latter is the capacity of your commitment. If you can't out-think 'em, out-hustle 'em.

To change one's life, start
immediately. Do it flamboyantly.
No exceptions.

—*William James*

Most people never change. Some change a little. A few change—flamboyantly! Be in the minority.

121

*Bad officials are elected by good
citizens who do not vote.*

—*anonymous*

Good government is hands-on. Exercise your right to participate: vote. And if you don't think that's enough, then run for office!

122

The minute you start talking about
what you're going to do if you lose,
you have lost.

—*George Schultz*

Don't rehearse losing; fixate on winning. Never waste time thinking about losing unless you've lost. Then learn from it.

123

Only dead fish swim with the stream.

—unknown

Fight the flow of mediocrity. Success always lies upstream.

Free enterprise will work if you will.

—*Ray Kroc*

The only admission to the system of free enterprise is one good idea coupled with the willingness to work hard.

The Distilled Wisdom Series

125

*Lord, grant that I may always desire
more than I can accomplish.*

—*Michelangelo*

The tee shirt says, "He who dies with the most toys wins." How about this: "He or she who dies with the most worthwhile projects in progress wins."

Never explain—your friends do not need it, and your enemies will not believe you anyway.

—Elbert Hubbard

Most explanations sound like excuses anyhow. Understand, but don't worry about explaining.

127

*When you like your work, every day
is a holiday.*

—*Frank Tyger*

The ideal job: There's no difference between what you do at work and what you do for fun, but somebody pays you for doing it anyhow.

Practice positive discontent. Be proud of what you've accomplished, but never be content with it.

—Mark Sanborn

This is a tricky one. The danger of contentment is that it creates complacency, and you quit striving. But if you never take time to savor what you've accomplished, striving won't ever be worthwhile. The key is to be content without being complacent.

129

I am convinced that one of the biggest factors in success is the courage to undertake something.

—*James A. Worsham*

Thinking, considering, wishing, con-templating, deciding, determining... none of them have the power of under-taking.

*Like people without worrying if they
are going to like you in return.*

—*Burt Reynolds*

Take this advice and you'll be astounded at how many people like you.

131

Those who stand for nothing will fall for anything.

—*unknown*

There is truth to be known. That's why they call it the truth. Seek it, and never believe those who say it's all a matter of opinion.

132

A half-truth is a whole lie.

—Edwin Louis Cole

Truth isn't a continuum; it's an either/or. The place between the "either" and the "or" is called a "lie."

133

You cannot suddenly fabricate foundations of strength. They must have been building all along.

—*Philip Yancey*

Character is developed slowly over time. Strength comes from hundreds of little but not insignificant acts of daily character building. You can deal better with the big things in life once you've learned the importance of handling the little things.

134

Work and associate with people who run at a fast pace.

—*Mark Sanborn*

If you want to learn more, hang out with those who learn well. If you want to be healthier, keep company with those who are committed to good health.

Associate with people who pull you up instead of put you down.

135

*You minus possessions
equals character.*

—*unknown*

How much of your sense of who you are is tied up with what you have?

136

The difference between excellence and mediocrity is the difference between common knowledge and consistent application.

—*Mark Sanborn*

Do a quick inventory: What are the five most important things that you know you could be doing to be more successful... but you aren't doing them? Before you learn more, make it a point to apply more.

137

The master is someone who stays on the mat five minutes longer than anybody else.

—Martial Arts saying

Here's a game I like to play with myself when I work out: After my last rep on the weight bench—when I'm completely exhausted—I try to do one more (make sure you've got a spotter if you do this yourself!). The lesson is clear: It takes just a little bit more to be a whole lot better.

138

*Live each day as if it were your last
and someday you'll be right.*

— unknown

Most of us never know when that last day will be and thinking we have many more, we lose a sense of urgency. Live each day like it were your last and even if it doesn't turn out that way, you'll be glad you did.

139

*I will work and get ready and
someday my chance will come.*

—*Abraham Lincoln*

This great leader's chance did come, and luckily he was ready when it did. Are you prepared for greatness? Heaven help you should the opportunity find you before you're ready to be found.

*Put yourself in the place of
maximum potential.*

—*Dewitt Jones*

Look for where things are happening. Go where exciting people are attempting worthwhile things and volunteer to help. Follow the action.

141

A lot of us in fast lane lifestyles are looking for the off-ramps.

—*David Zach*

And sometimes the ones who can't find the off-ramps crash. Know the appropriate speed limits in your own life.

For where your treasure is, there will your heart be also.

—Matthew 6:21

Where you spend your time and money will also tell you where your heart is. It has been said that immorality is loving things and using people; morality is loving people and using things.

143

There is only one success—to be able to spend your life in your own way.

—*Christoper Morley*

I can define the word "success" but only you can define *your* success.

Our life is what our thoughts make it.

— *Marcus Aurelius*

Your thoughts are the seeds of your destiny. It is through cultivating your thoughts that you grow your future.

145

*It's a great satisfaction knowing that
for a brief point in time
you made a difference.*

—*Irene Natividad*

We all make a difference. The question is, what kind?

146

There are two things to aim at in life: first, to get what you want; and after that, to enjoy it. Only the wisest of mankind achieve the second.

—Logan Pearsall Smith

How much is enough? To most, the answer is always, "Just a little bit more." Don't try to get more of what you want until you learn to enjoy more of what you've already got.

147

He never grew up but he never stopped growing.

—*What Arthur Clarke wants as his epitaph*

I, like Clarke, want to be child-like without being childish. If you never lose your sense of wonder, you'll never stop growing.

148

*Those who learn fastest will achieve
more than those who learn best.*

—*Paul Zane Pilzer*

The world changes so rapidly that
we must be able to learn rapidly just to
keep up. By the time you've learned
something thoroughly, it may no longer
be important. Learn well, but learn
quickly.

The Distilled Wisdom Series

149

The ultimate of being successful is the luxury of giving yourself the time to do what you want to do.

—*Leontyne Price*

Reward yourself with an enjoyment break. Take the next 30 minutes to do something you really want to do. The stuff you need to do will wait for you.

150

The most overlooked area of personal achievement is balance. A person must not be considered successful if either the professional or personal arenas are unsatisfying.

— Scott McKain

Don't choose between personal and professional success; choose both. One without the other is neither.

151

*When you come to a fork
in the road, take it.*

—*Yogi Berra*

What a crazy, zany, nutty, weird and wonderful world. Make your sense of humor your constant companion.

Take what you do in this life
seriously, but don't take yourself
too seriously.

—*Mark Sanborn*

Laugh and the world laughs with you. Take yourself too seriously and the world laughs at you. Tell more jokes, play more pranks, loosen up more and have a blast for the rest of the trip.

Mark Sanborn is known as the high-content speaker who motivates. He addresses audiences throughout the United States and internationally on leadership, customer service, teambuilding and mastering change. He has authored numerous audios, videos, books and other learning resources. For more information about Mark's speeches, seminars or learning resources, please contact him at:

Sanborn & Associates, Inc.
677 S. Williams
Denver, CO 80209
(800) 650-EDGE
fax (303) 777-3045
internet: MarkSpeaks@aol.com

INDEX